THE KANSAS CITY CHIEFS

BY JOANNE MATTERN

EPIC

EPIC BOOKS are no ordinary books. They burst with intense action, high-speed heroics, and shadows of the unknown. Are you ready for an Epic adventure?

This book is intended for educational use. Organization and franchise logos are trademarks of the National Football League (NFL). This is not an official book of the NFL. It is not approved by or connected with the NFL.

This edition first published in 2024 by Bellwether Media, Inc.

No part of this publication may be reproduced in whole or in part without written permission of the publisher. For information regarding permission, write to Bellwether Media, Inc., Attention: Permissions Department, 6012 Blue Circle Drive, Minnetonka, MN 55343.

Library of Congress Cataloging-in-Publication Data

Names: Mattern, Joanne, 1963- author.
Title: The Kansas City Chiefs / by Joanne Mattern.
Description: Minneapolis, MN : Bellwether Media, 2024. | Series: Epic. NFL team profiles | Includes bibliographical references and index. | Audience: Ages 7-12 | Audience: Grades 2-3 | Summary: "Engaging images accompany information about the Kansas City Chiefs. The combination of high-interest subject matter and light text is intended for students in grades 2 through 7"-- Provided by publisher.
Identifiers: LCCN 2023021958 (print) | LCCN 2023021959 (ebook) | ISBN 9798886874815 (library binding) | ISBN 9798886876697 (ebook)
Subjects: LCSH: Kansas City Chiefs (Football team)--History--Juvenile literature.
Classification: LCC GV956.K35 M37 2024 (print) | LCC GV956.K35 (ebook) | DDC 796.332/6409778411--dc23/eng/20230517
LC record available at https://lccn.loc.gov/2023021958
LC ebook record available at https://lccn.loc.gov/2023021959

Text copyright © 2024 by Bellwether Media, Inc. EPIC and associated logos are trademarks and/or registered trademarks of Bellwether Media, Inc.

Editor: Betsy Rathburn   Designer: Jeffrey Kollock

Printed in the United States of America, North Mankato, MN.

TABLE OF CONTENTS

A BIG COMEBACK!	4
THE HISTORY OF THE CHIEFS	6
THE CHIEFS TODAY	14
GAME DAY!	16
KANSAS CITY CHIEFS FACTS	20
GLOSSARY	22
TO LEARN MORE	23
INDEX	24

A BIG COMEBACK!

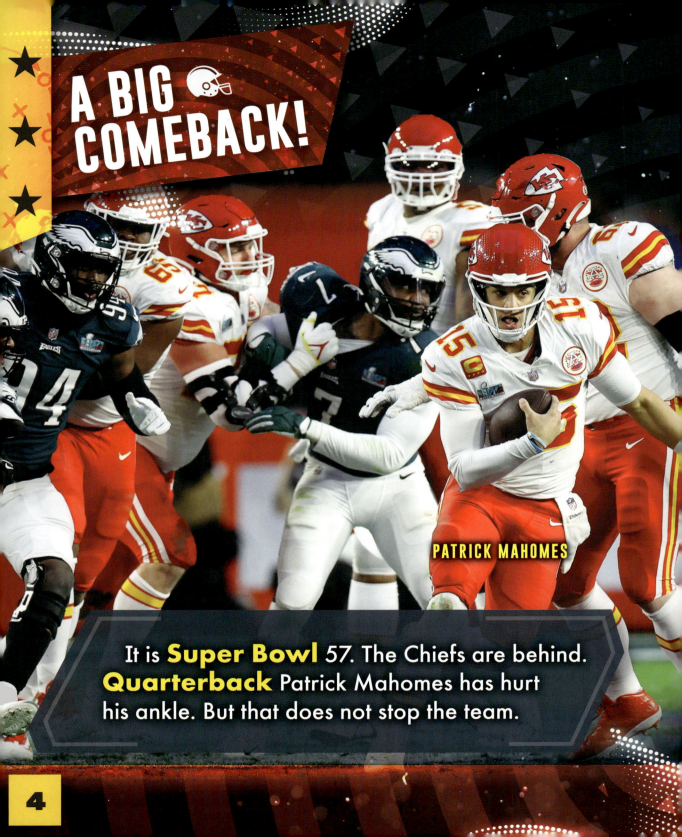

PATRICK MAHOMES

It is **Super Bowl** 57. The Chiefs are behind. **Quarterback** Patrick Mahomes has hurt his ankle. But that does not stop the team.

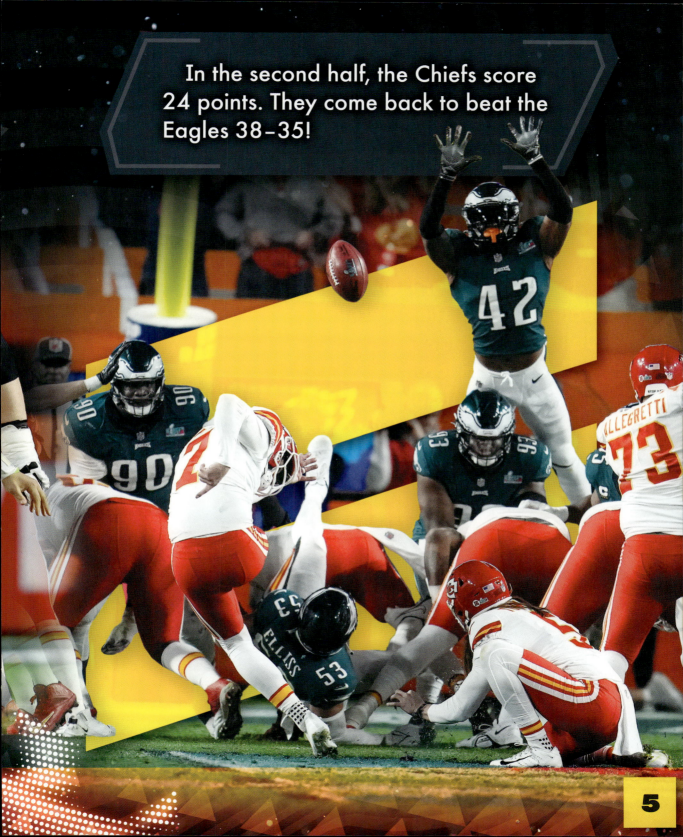

In the second half, the Chiefs score 24 points. They come back to beat the Eagles 38–35!

THE HISTORY OF THE CHIEFS

In 1960, Lamar Hunt started a football team in Texas. They were called the Dallas Texans.

Three years later, the Texans moved to Kansas City, Missouri. They changed their name to the Kansas City Chiefs.

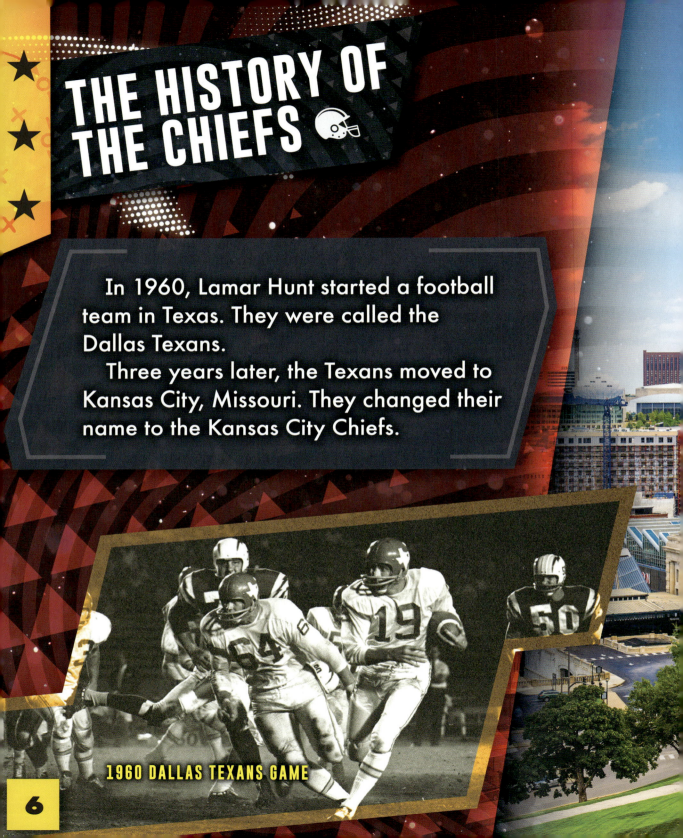

1960 DALLAS TEXANS GAME

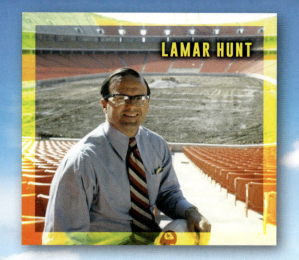

LAMAR HUNT

JOINED TOGETHER

The Chiefs were first part of the American Football League (AFL). The AFL joined the National Football League (NFL) in 1970.

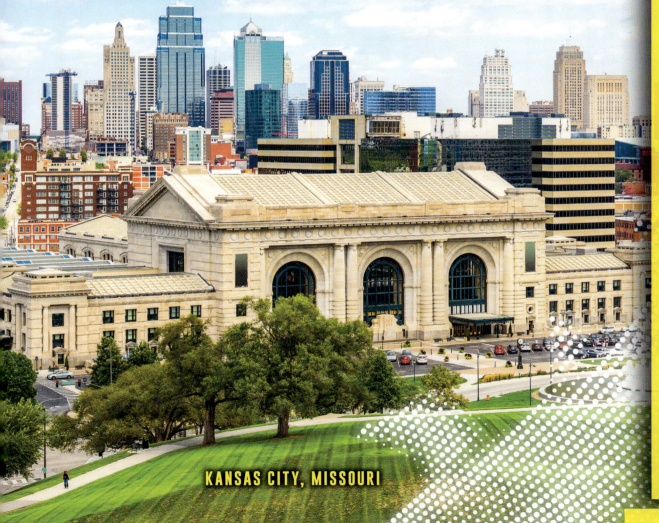

KANSAS CITY, MISSOURI

SUPER BOWL 1

The Chiefs were a great team. In 1967, they played in the first Super Bowl! They lost to the Green Bay Packers.

SUPER BOWL 4

They were Super Bowl **champions** three years later. They beat the Minnesota Vikings 23–7!

The Chiefs struggled in the 1970s and 1980s. But their luck turned around in the 1990s. They made the **playoffs** many times.

TONY GONZALEZ

They had many strong players. **Tight end** Tony Gonzalez joined the team in 1997. He set many NFL records!

TROPHY CASE

AFL championships
3

AFC championships
3

SUPER BOWL championships
3

AFC WEST championships
13

The Chiefs made the playoffs six times between 2000 and 2016. In 2017, the team **drafted** Patrick Mahomes.

PATRICK MAHOMES IN 2017

Mahomes led the team to win Super Bowl 54 in 2020. In 2023, the Chiefs won the Super Bowl again!

SUPER BOWL 54

THE CHIEFS TODAY

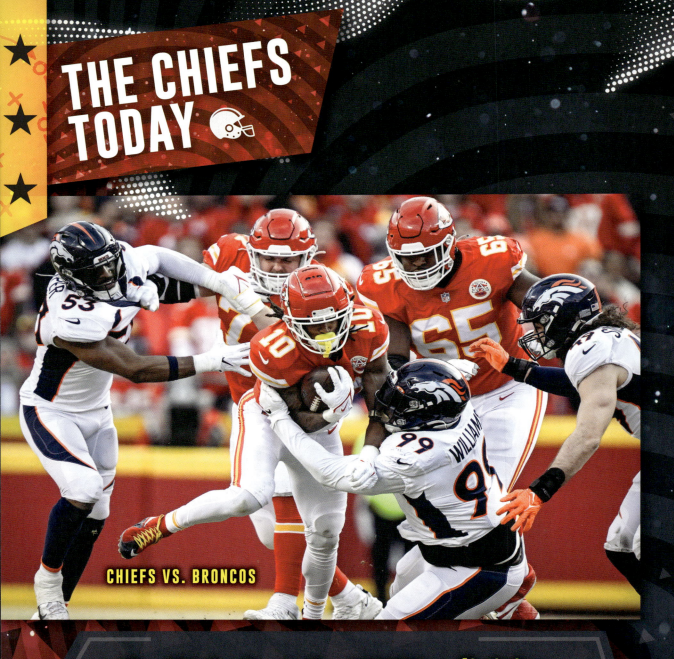

CHIEFS VS. BRONCOS

The Chiefs play in the AFC West **division**. They play at Arrowhead **Stadium** in Kansas City, Missouri.

14

The Denver Broncos and the Las Vegas Raiders are the Chiefs' top **rivals**.

LOCATION

ARROWHEAD STADIUM
Kansas City, Missouri

MISSOURI

GAME DAY!

Chiefs fans love their team! Fans wear red, gold, and white on game day.
They cheer loudly when the Chiefs make a good play. Arrowhead Stadium is the loudest stadium in the NFL!

ARROWHEAD STADIUM

LOUD AND PROUD

In 2014, Chiefs fans set the Guinness World Record for loudest crowd at a sports stadium!

17

The team's **mascot** is a big part of every game. KC Wolf dances and waves flags. Fans go wild when they see KC. They love to cheer for the Kansas City Chiefs!

HALL OF FAMER

KC Wolf is the oldest active NFL mascot. He is part of the National Mascot Hall of Fame!

KC WOLF

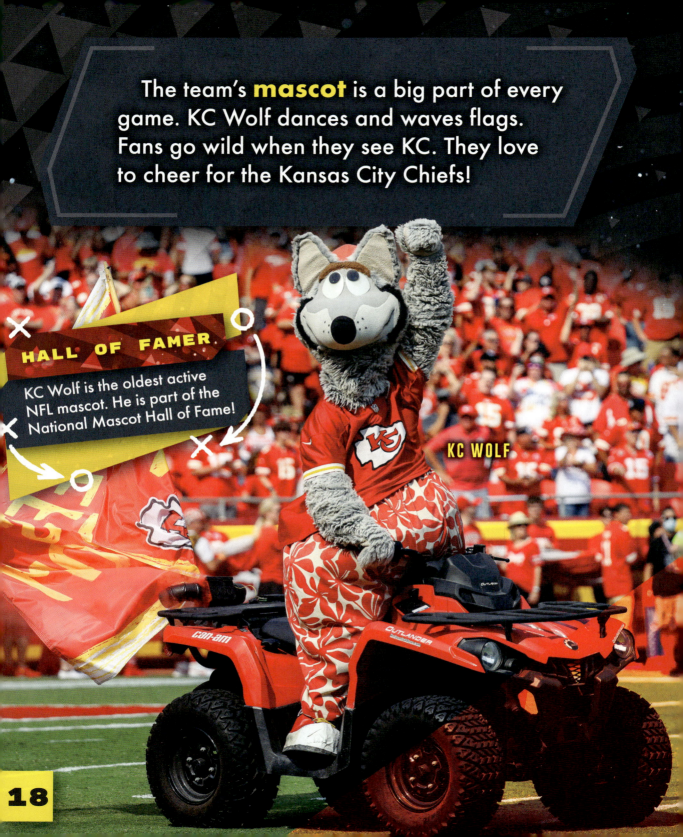

KANSAS CITY CHIEFS FACTS

LOGO

JOINED THE NFL | **1970** (AFL 1960–1969)

NICKNAME | None

MASCOT: KC WOLF

CONFERENCE | American Football Conference (AFC)

COLORS

DIVISION | AFC West

 Denver Broncos

 Las Vegas Raiders

 Los Angeles Chargers

STADIUM

ARROWHEAD STADIUM
opened August 12, 1972

holds **76,416** people

20

⏱ TIMELINE

1960
The Kansas City Chiefs begin as the Dallas Texans

1970
The Chiefs win their first Super Bowl

2023
The Chiefs win their third Super Bowl

1963
The team moves to Kansas City

2020
The Chiefs win their second Super Bowl

★ RECORDS ★

All-Time Interceptions Leader

Emmitt Thomas
58 interceptions

All-Time Rushing Leader

Jamaal Charles
7,260 yards

Single-Season Rushing Leader

Larry Johnson
1,789 yards in 2006

All-Time Scoring Leader

Nick Lowery
1,466 points

21

GLOSSARY

champions—winners of a contest that decides the best team or person

division—a group of NFL teams from the same area that often play against each other; there are eight divisions in the NFL.

drafted—chose a college athlete to play for a professional team

mascot—an animal or symbol that represents a sports team

playoffs—games played after the regular season is over; playoff games determine which teams play in the championship game.

quarterback—a player whose main job is to throw and hand off the ball

rivals—long-standing opponents

stadium—an arena where sports are played

Super Bowl—the annual championship game of the NFL

tight end—a player whose main jobs are to catch the ball and block for teammates

TO LEARN MORE

AT THE LIBRARY

Abdo, Kenny. *Kansas City Chiefs*. Minneapolis, Minn.: Abdo Zoom, 2022.

Corso, Phil. *Patrick Mahomes*. New York, N.Y.: PowerKids Press, 2022.

Whiting, Jim. *The Story of the Kansas City Chiefs*. Mankato, Minn.: Creative Education, 2019.

ON THE WEB

FACTSURFER

Factsurfer.com gives you a safe, fun way to find more information.

1. Go to www.factsurfer.com.

2. Enter "Kansas City Chiefs" into the search box and click 🔍.

3. Select your book cover to see a list of related content.

INDEX

AFC West, 14, 20

American Football League (AFL), 7, 20

Arrowhead Stadium, 14, 15, 16, 17, 20

colors, 16, 20

famous players, 19

fans, 16, 17, 18

Gonzalez, Tony, 10, 11

Guinness World Record, 17

history, 4, 5, 6, 7, 8, 9, 10, 11, 12, 13

Hunt, Lamar, 6, 7

Kansas City, Missouri, 6, 7, 14, 15

Kansas City Chiefs facts, 20–21

Mahomes, Patrick, 4, 12, 13

mascot, 18, 20

name, 6

National Football League (NFL), 7, 11, 16, 18, 20

playoffs, 10, 12

positions, 4, 11

records, 11, 21

rivals, 15

Super Bowl, 4, 5, 8, 9, 13

Texas, 6

timeline, 21

trophy case, 11

The images in this book are reproduced through the courtesy of: G. Newman Lowrance/ AP Images, front cover, pp. 1, 18-19; Paparacy, front cover (stadium), pp. 1, 15 (stadium); Sipa USA/ Alamy, p. 3; Gregory Shamus/ Staff/ Getty Images, p. 4; Marcio J. Sanchez/ AP Images, p. 5; The Enthusiast Network/ Contributor/ Getty Images, pp. 6, 21 (1960); Sean Pavone, pp. 6-7; Kansas City Chiefs/ Wikipedia, p. 7 (inset); James Flores/ Contributor/ Getty Images, pp. 8, 19 (Len Dawson); Focus On Sport/ Contributor/ Getty Images, pp. 9, 19 (Bobby Bell), 21 (Nick Lowery); Icon Sports Wire/ Contributor/ Getty Images, pp. 10-11, 12-13, 20 (mascot); Tribune Content Agency LLC/ Alamy, pp. 12, 19 (Patrick Mahomes); AAron Ontiveroz/ MediaNews Group/ The Denver Post via Getty Images/ Contributor/ Getty Images, p. 14; NFL/ Wikipedia, pp. 15 (logo), 20 (logos); David Eulitt/ Contributor/ Getty Images, p. 16; Reed Hoffmann/ AP Images, pp. 16-17; Rich Kane Photography/ Alamy, p. 19 (Derrick Thomas); Abaca Press/ Alamy, p. 19 (Tony Gonzalez); Katherine Welles, p. 20 (stadium); f11photo, p. 21 (1963); Kansas City Star/ Contributor/ Getty Images, p. 21 (1970); Al Bello/ Staff/ Getty Images, p. 21 (2020); Ezra Shaw/ Staff/ Getty Images, p. 21 (2023); Lou Witt/ AP Images, p. 21 (Emmitt Thomas); ZUMA Press Inc/ Alamy, p. 21 (Jamaal Charles); David Stluka/ AP Images, p. 21 (Larry Johnson); UPI/ Alamy, p. 23.